Fishers
Then and Now

Lisa Zamosky

Contributing Author
Jill K. Mulhall, M.Ed.

Associate Editor
Christina Hill, M.A.

Assistant Editor
Torrey Maloof

Editorial Director
Emily R. Smith, M.A.Ed.

Project Researcher
Gillian Eve Makepeace

Editor-in-Chief
Sharon Coan, M.S.Ed.

Editorial Manager
Gisela Lee, M.A.

Creative Director
Lee Aucoin

Illustration Manager
Timothy J. Bradley

Designers
Lesley Palmer
Debora Brown
Zac Calbert
Robin Erickson

Project Consultant
Corinne Burton, M.A.Ed.

Publisher
Rachelle Cracchiolo, M.S.Ed.

Teacher Created Materials Publishing

5301 Oceanus Drive
Huntington Beach, CA 92649
http://www.tcmpub.com
ISBN 978-0-7439-9378-4

Table of Contents

One of the Oldest Jobs in the World

Fishing was one of the world's first jobs. Early fishers had to work hard to find only a few fish. Then, they learned ways to make their jobs easier. They created new tools. They used boats to go out in the water. Now, fishers catch enough fish to feed the whole world.

▼ An Indian fishing in a stream

An ➡ Asian fish market

⬇ Fishers working on a boat

This boy is pulling a net full of crawfish.

Look at all the crawfish in this bin!

Easy Fishing

Shellfish are the easiest fish to catch. Lobsters (LAWB-stuhrz), crabs, and shrimp are types of shellfish. They do not swim fast. People first caught them with traps and nets. They fished in lakes and rivers. Fishers went where the water was shallow.

This is a trap. It can catch lobsters and crabs.

Fishing Tools

The earliest fishers used knives to catch fish. Then, they learned to use other tools like nets and spears. Later, they tried fishhooks, fish lines, and **lures**.

At first, fishers would fish from the shore. Later, fishers began to use boats to go out in the water. They found more fish. They also caught bigger fish.

These lures are used to catch fish.

◄ This man uses a spear to fish from a boat.

▲ Otter catching a fish

Animals Helping

In China, otters are trained to dive for fish. They help the fishers catch fish. In Japan, the fishers train birds to help them catch fish.

▼ Big nets help catch a lot of fish.

Saving the Fish

Fishers now had better tools. So, they caught more fish than they could eat right away. They had to learn to **harvest** (HAWR-vuhst) the fish. They had to keep the extra fish from going bad. So, they salted, dried, and smoked the fish. This kept it from being ruined.

The fishers did not need all the fish for their families. So, they sold the extra fish in markets.

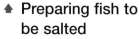
▲ Preparing fish to be salted

◄ Salting fish below a boat's deck

Pets Need Fish, Too

Three out of ten fish caught are not for us to eat. They are used to feed pets and farm animals.

◀ Fish drying in the sun

▼ Fish drying in the sea wind

Fishing Boats

Over time, boats got bigger. They took fishers further out to sea. They also helped fishers harvest more fish. Early boats were called **sailboats**. They were powered by the wind. But, if there was no wind, the boats would just drift. Later, **steamships** took the place of sailboats. They could travel far in any kind of weather.

▼ Fishers on a sailboat fishing

⬆ In the 1880s, fish were bought and sold here.

⬇ This is a steamship.

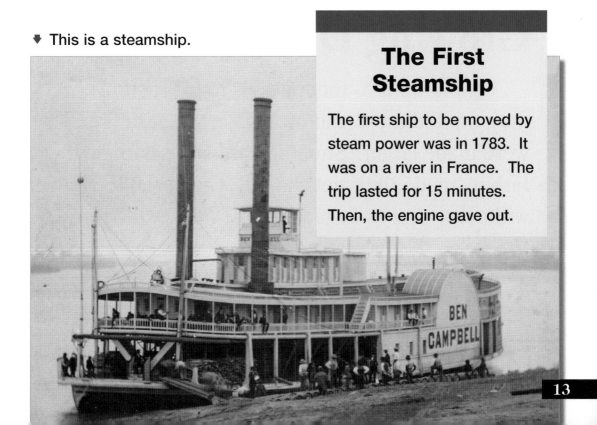

The First Steamship

The first ship to be moved by steam power was in 1783. It was on a river in France. The trip lasted for 15 minutes. Then, the engine gave out.

Growing Demand

People went to the **markets** to buy fish. Soon, they wanted more and more fish. So, fishing boats were made larger. Small fish traps were made bigger. Fishers made their nets larger. They used long lines with many hooks instead of just one.

Fish in Demand

People love to eat fish. Nearly 130 million (MIL-yuhn) tons of fish are caught each year. That's a lot of fish!

◀ This boat drags a large net to catch many fish at once.

Look at all the ▶
traps lined up
on the dock!

◀ Fishing net being carried to shore

Hiring More Help

The new tools helped fishers catch more fish. But these tools were harder to use. More people were needed to make them work. So, fishers hired people to help on their boats. The fishing **industry** (IN-duhs-tree) grew.

Hooks used ➡ to catch fish

⬅ This captain steers his boat.

This fisher holds ➡ his catch.

Dangerous Job

Fishing can be a very dangerous (DAYN-juhr-uhs) job. The tools are sharp. The boats move fast and are slippery. Fishers have to be careful. If they do not pay attention to what they are doing, they might get hurt.

Stronger Boats

Boats began to be built with motors. Motorboats were better than the other fishing boats. Boats with motors could travel far out to sea. They could stay there for days or even weeks. The fishers could catch more fish.

Boats used to be made out of wood. Today, most large fishing boats are made of steel. These boats are much stronger.

New steel boats ➤ are very strong.

⬆ Fishers with their day's catch

Refrigerator on Board

Fishing boats have containers in them called **holds**. The holds are kept cold. Fishers put the fish they catch in the holds. This keeps the fish from going bad.

⬇ These fish are being put in the hold.

This captain uses ➡ a computer on his boat.

Catch for Sale

Today, there are a lot of fishers. Fishing is now a big **business** (BIZ-nuhs). **Fisheries** (FIH-shuh-reez) sell all kinds of fish.

Most fishing boats now have computers. They are great tools for fishers. They help captains see what kind of weather is coming. And, they help the fishers find the best fishing spots. This makes the work of a fisher much easier.

Protecting the Fish

Many kinds of fish are now **extinct** (ik-STINGKT). Fishers caught too many of them. Now, they are gone. Today, there are laws to stop this. Some fish cannot be caught at all. Other kinds can only be caught at certain times.

◄ Fishers today have rules to follow.

▼ These women pack fish eggs into glass jars.

Bringing in the Fish

Some fishers spend days at sea. Then, they sail their boats back to the harbor. They unpack their catch and put it on ice. The fish goes right to the market.

Millions of people eat fish every day. We rely on fishers to catch the fish we need. Fishing is an important job.

▼ A fish market in 1900

▲ A fish market today

Have you ever been fishing? If so, then you know that it is hard work. Fishers have to be patient. Then, they have to take the fish they catch to the markets. The next time you see seafood in a store, think about a fisher's job. It took a lot of work for that fish to be ready for sale.

A Day in the Life Then

Ahrookoos (1851–1899)

Ahrookoos (UH-roo-kooz) was a Hupa Indian. He lived in California (kal-uh-FORN-yuh) by the Trinity River. His people fished for food. They used spears and nets to catch salmon. His tribe had many songs and dances. He was a good fisher.

Let's pretend to ask Ahrookoos some questions about his job.

Why did you decide to be a fisher?

My tribe needs to eat. I help feed my people. It is a special job. Some people in our tribe are not strong enough to catch fish.

That is why I do it. I am good at catching fish. But, it is also a hard job.

What is your day like?

In the morning I get my canoe (kuh-NEW) ready for the day. I put my fishing tools in the boat. On the river, I fish for salmon with my spear. I bring all the fish back to my tribe. At night, we cook the fish in baskets we make. We also eat acorn flour and deer. At night, we sing and dance. I am very tired when I go to bed.

What do you like most about your job?

I am important to my people. They need me to catch fish for food. I help my tribe stay healthy and strong. That makes me feel special.

Tools of the Trade Then

This fisher had to use a small ▶
net to catch fish. He made the
net himself. He did not have a
boat. So, he had to walk across
the bridge until he caught a fish.

◀ These fishers used big nets
on a fishing boat. This is
how they caught **oysters**.

This is a **tackle box** ▶
from long ago.
It belonged to
George Washington.
He used it to carry
his fishing tools.

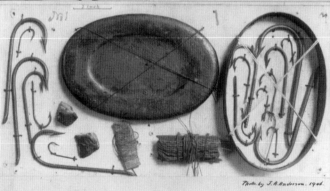

Washington's Fishing Tackle.

Tools of the Trade Now

◆ Today, fishers use big nets. They take boats far out to sea. These fishers have caught tons of shrimp and fish!

Fishers also use fishing poles to catch ➤ fish. A pole has a piece of string with a hook at the end. The fish gets caught on the hook. Then, the fisher winds up the string and pulls the fish onto the boat.

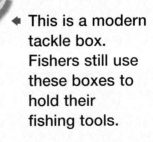

◆ This is a modern tackle box. Fishers still use these boxes to hold their fishing tools.

A Day in the Life Now

John Levins

John Levins is a fisherman. He fishes in Louisiana (loo-ee-zee-AN-uh). His job is hard work. He has to fish in all kinds of weather. But, he loves it. Mr. Levins has been fishing for 35 years.

⬆ Mr. Levins proudly holds his catch of the day.

Why did you decide to become a fisher?

My Uncle Lee was a fisherman. He took me to his catfish traps. I was only seven years old. I remember all of the smells. I remember the smell of his rain suit. And, I remember the smell of the bait. I loved the smell of the fresh, clean air coming over the water. You could almost taste it. We would fish early in the morning. The colors outside in the morning were so bright. It was beautiful.

I liked to pick up the traps and see all the fish wiggle. And, I loved to ride on boats.

What is your day like?

A bad day fishing is better than a good day doing anything else. I wake up early. I am excited to see what I will catch. The work is very hard! I have to be careful. I work with sharp hooks and ropes. It is a real challenge. I have to know about the weather and the **tides**. And, I have to know the air and water **temperatures** (TEMP-uhr-uh-churz). These things help me know where the fish will be and if they will be hungry that day.

What do you like most about your job?

The thrill of the catch makes fishing a great job. And, I like the freedom of each day. When I am on my boat, I feel like I am part of nature. I notice everything around me. And, that makes me feel good.

Glossary

business—the buying and selling of goods

extinct—when something is no longer living on Earth

fisheries—fishing businesses

harvest—to take fish from a sea, lake, or river and sell for food

holds—storage containers in the bottom of ships

industry—the making and selling of food or other things

lures—fake bait with hooks; used to catch fish

markets—places for buying and selling things

oysters—a type of shellfish

sailboats—boats that move through water using only the wind in their sails

shellfish—an animal from the ocean that has a shell

steamships—large boats that are pushed through the water using steam power

tackle box—a small box used to hold fishing tools

temperatures—levels of hot and cold

tides—the rising and falling of the ocean

Index

Credits

Acknowledgements

Special thanks to John Levins for providing the *Day in the Life Now* interview. Mr. Levins is a fisherman in Louisiana.

Image Credits

cover John and Frankie Levins; p.1 John and Frankie Levins; p.4 (left) Ed George/National Geographic/Getty Images; p.4 (right) Photos.com; p.5 (top) Photos.com; p.5 (bottom) Photos.com; p.6 (top) John and Frankie Levins; p.6 (bottom) John and Frankie Levins; pp.6–7 (top) Photos.com; pp.6–7 (bottom) Photos.com; p.8 (top left) Photos.com; p.8 (top right) Photos.com; p.8 (bottom left) Photos.com; p.8 (bottom right) Photos.com; p.9 (top) Photos.com; p.9 (bottom) Photos.com; p.10 (top) The Library of Congress; p.10 (bottom) The Library of Congress; p.11 (top) iStockphoto.com/Ronald Hoiting; p.11 (bottom) Photos.com; p.12 The Library of Congress; p.13 (top) North Wind Picture Archives; p.13 (bottom) The Library of Congress; p.14 (top) Vera Bogaerts/Shutterstock, Inc.; pp.14–15 Photos.com; p.15 Denis Pepin/Shutterstock, Inc.; p.16 Photo Researchers; p.17 (top) Photos.com; p.17 (bottom) John and Frankie Levins; pp.18–19 Yare Marketing/Shutterstock, Inc.; p.19 (top) Getty Images; p.19 (bottom) Getty Images; p.20 Getty Images; p.21 (top) John and Frankie Levins; p.21 (bottom) Getty Images; p.22 Getty Images; p.23 (top) Mark Yuill/Shutterstock, Inc.; p.23 (bottom) Stephen Walls/Shutterstock, Inc.; p.24 The Library of Congress; p.25 The Library of Congress; p.26 (top) The Library of Congress; p.26 (middle) The Library of Congress; p.26 (bottom) The Library of Congress; p.27 (top) Photos.com; p.27 (middle) Julia Gequillana/Shutterstock Inc.; p.27 (bottom) Photos.com; p.28 Courtesy of John Levins; p.29 Courtesy of John Levins; back cover The Library of Congress